novum pro

Jacques Huinck

TO THINK
OR
TO
MARCH

a handy reference book
for lovers of peace

novum pro

© 2022 novum publishing

ISBN 978-1-64268-212-0
Cover photos: Frantic00 | Dreamstime.com,
Jacques Huinck
Cover design, layout & typesetting:
novum publishing
Internal illustrations: Jacques Huinck

The images provided by the author have
been printed in the highest possible quality.

www.novumpublishing.com

All rights of distribution,
including via film, radio, and television,
photomechanical reproduction,
audio storage media, electronic data
storage media, and the reprinting of
portions of text, are reserved.

1. Fort Saint Pieter.

"Ladies and gentlemen, first of all I would like to introduce myself. My name is Jacques. I am a guide of the Fort, and after this extensive life description, I will open the door for you."

With these immensely funny words, my tour in the Fort St. Pieter in Maastricht always started. I became a guide there after my retirement.

Next, I congratulated everyone who had been born after 1960, because before that year, life all over the world had been extremely miserable. The cause of that was the fact that the pill did not yet exist. Every young couple had in no time, eight, twelve, or fifteen children. Johann Sebastian Bach even had twenty-one children, but he had a good income. Most people did not, so their poverty increased year after year. They had no money to maintain their houses, so they became slum dwellings, and their streets became backstreets. Parents had no time to raise so many children, and they became street children, who didn't go to school. No time for this nonsense! They had to struggle for their daily food.

2.   Panic.

Because nobody had any time to think, the corn on the fields was mowed with a scythe, a typical illiterate invention. Because of that, the harvest was often scanty, and famine was always lurking. There was also the problem of the insects who tried to run away with the harvest. They were fought with holy water and Latin prayers—again, an invention of ignorant, distraught people.

If the harvest was really too small, then panic arose in the area.

Panic arises when you are in a situation where you can get hurt or sick or risk dying. This leads to a flood of adrenaline in your blood. This homemade hard drug is good for the muscles but bad for the brain. It makes good-natured people fierce and dangerous, so they lose their self-control and their ability to think clearly or do anything.

When that kind of thing happened on a large scale, all these adrenaline sufferers ran out of their houses to smash stones through the windows in their streets and destroy as much as possible.

It didn't help at all, but their brains had been switched off by the poison of adrenaline.

Well-fed kings, seeing these scenes from the windows of their palace, wondered what to do with those people.

They used an old trick and said to the boys (who were the strongest and therefore the most dangerous), "Boys, come join my army! I have beautiful uniforms for you. The girls like that very much! And there, at the horizon, is where the enemy lives. He is to blame for everything. You are allowed to destroy everything there, but please don't do it here."

And so, an innocent community suddenly saw an army of dangerous savages approaching, in beautiful uniforms, sent by a relieved king.

In addition to sudden life-threatening events such as hunger, you can also get adrenaline poisoning in a slow, almost sneaky way.

Chronic lack of money and living for years in a slum house with a clogged toilet in the company of hungry mice can produce a nice amount of adrenaline.

Psychological threats can also generate adrenaline.

Being chronically ignored and humiliated has the same effect.

When torments approach slowly, the panic feeling grows slower as well, but once the measure is full, than the adrenaline bomb bursts. A small incident is then enough to get a frustrated crowd out of their homes to smash windows.

This phenomenon can occur in any country and has nothing to do with nationality or race.

Afterwards, those people are ashamed of what they have done, but they were no longer themselves. Their brains were paralyzed by the drug of adrenaline.

3. Roman adrenalin.

Already in Roman times, corn was mowed with primitive sickles, with occasional famine as a result. Then the old song was heard again: hunger / panic / adrenaline / blind rage / leader points to the horizon where 'the enemy' lives who is blamed for everything / the extermination begins / end-result: more hunger.

What did the Romans do after they punished and defeated all of their so-called enemies? Return home?

"Not at all!" was shouted in shock by the people in Rome.

A smart Roman came up with the idea of having the Roman army build roads. Europe is full of them. Large, heavy stones were nicely cut into rectangular blocks. As long as the Roman street fighters, plagued by misery, so full of adrenaline and aggression, were busy with these roads, they were rid of them in Rome.

Of course, these road builders caused a birth wave in the surrounding villages as a side effect, but that wave moved as work on the roads moved. (Unlike the case of the pyramid builders.)

And so around the year zero, the Romans arrived at the river Maas, where Maastricht is now located. Part of the Roman army remained there while the rest of them moved, making roads and children along the way, to Cologne, while the people in Rome were still very relieved.

At the place where the Romans stayed at the Maas, they built a tent camp called "Mosa Trajectum" (later corrupted to Maastricht).

At that place, you could easily wade through the Maas because the river was wider there and therefore less deep. They found it unnecessary to build a wall around their camp. A vicious dog was cheaper.

But the local natives were dressed in drafty bear skins, had goosebumps from cold, and were weak from hunger. The life threats they faced filled them with adrenaline that crippled their brains to the level of foot-stamping toddlers.

So they gave the dog a kick and destroyed the Roman settlement. After the massacre that followed, the Romans built a 'castellum.' This was a village surrounded by a wall that contained ten towers and two gate buildings. On the other side of the Maas, on the east side, they made a smaller castellum, and a bridge was built between those two reinforcements.

Was that all necessary? Yes, to protect them from the barbarians (the soldiers were told) but primarily to keep the soldiers (adrenaline sufferers from Roman slums) as long as possible out of their country. That worked until around the year 400 when they went back home.

Dear reader, this booklet is not about the history of Maastricht. This city only serves as a test tube. The same things happened in dozens of European cities. I describe the causes and misery of wars, but while writing I also found some solutions. That will be useful, I hope.

Think with me! I am not infallible. Correct me. That is how we move forward together.

4. A new bridge.

The empty homes that the Romans left in Maastricht were quickly taken by the local population, which had meanwhile developed somewhat, after a 400-year Roman example. Bearskins had been out of fashion for years. With such ridiculous clothes, you could no longer walk the streets without being laughed at.

Because the village of Maastricht continued to grow, more and more people had to live outside the walls that the Romans built. It was already the year 1100, so it was high time to make the city wall larger.

Just when they had saved enough money, the old Roman bridge collapsed. Nobody had realized that bridges needed maintenance. It happened during a procession, and many people drowned. After that shock, people decided that the savings intended for a larger city wall had to be used for the construction of a new bridge. That became the Servaas Bridge in the Romanesque style (a style copied from the Romans). The larger city wall was built several years later.

5. New walls.

The new city wall was an extremely solid structure, recognizable by the brown natural stone. They called it 'the first wall' (nobody wanted to remember the broken Roman wall). This safe wall attracted many new residents to the city. Result: within a hundred years, Maastricht was so overcrowded by around 1200 that a larger wall had to be built. It was made of gray Namur stone and was higher and thicker than the first. The second wall had forty towers and five gates, and the city became four times as large. A piece of agricultural land was also reserved within that second wall so that the residents had something to eat during long sieges. (This became the gardens of the Beyard monastery.)

Again, everyone was happy with this solid wall, but not for long, because a Chinese invention came to Europe: the cannon! By standing in front of a city wall with a row of cannons and shooting at exactly the same spot the wall could collapse. It took a lot of patience to hit the same spot with such a primitive cannon, but in the end it worked. So the people of Maastricht decided not to wait to be attacked. They reinforced the back of the new city wall with a clay embankment about twenty meters thick.

6. Louis XIV is coming to Maastricht.

For the sake of convenience, I will skip a dozen sieges of Maastricht (including one by Spanish soldiers who were very, very poisoned by adrenaline and so extra dangerous).

In 1673, once again there was a food shortage in Paris. To get all those adrenaline sufferers out of the country, Louis XIV decided to conquer Liège and Maastricht "to give France more room." That sounded nice and caring. The soldiers (and historians) had to believe that something noble was being done here. In no case should the soldiers discover the truth: that they, with their fear for starvation and therefore their dangerous adrenaline poisoning, were considered a sort of plague sufferers who had to be dressed in uniforms and sent abroad as quickly as possible.

The French king Louis XIV, who was probably bored by his wealth, came with his army to Maastricht. He wanted to see how his soldiers would conquer such a city.

In his army was an engineer named Vauban. Unfortunately, Vauban had to inform his majesty that the city wall of Maastricht was so reinforced that no cannonball could break through it.

"But," Vauban said, "I found the weak point: the gate Tongersepoort."

You couldn't just shoot at that gate because there were thick walls in front of it, and you had to walk zigzag to reach the gate. People can do that, but cannonballs cannot.

"No," said the engineer. "We're going to shoot that gate from out of the sky!"

"The sky?" the king asked, surprised.

"Yes," said Vauban. "I mean from the St. Pietersberg." This is a hill on the south side of the town from about 120 meters high.

The French lined up a row of 18 cannons on the edge of the St. Pietersberg and shot for the next three weeks from there toward the Tongersepoort. Most cannonballs missed it, but in the end by chance the gate was struck a few times and collapsed. Then the French street fighters ran screeching into the city to perform good works, as it will undoubtedly be recorded in French history books.

After five years, the vacation was over. Paris was no longer experiencing hunger. Adrenaline levels sank, people could think and laugh again, and the French army was welcomed home with great fanfare. Rightly so, since they had done much good for France by being absent. The heavily damaged town of Maastricht was given back to the rightful owners with excuses for the inconvenience. After all, it was therapy, and one must take that into consideration.

When the French army withdrew, one man was baffled: engineer Vauban. He had been busy trying to strengthen the city of Maastricht with extensive anti-cannon fortifications. This led to him barking out a number of curses, in which undoubtedly a lot of saints and genitals were incorporated.

Maastricht would become a French city, he was always told.

"Could that piece of majesty have not said that a bit earlier?"

Did Vauban really say that? No, because he did not want to be beheaded (according to the rough habits of that time), but no doubt he thought something along those lines.

The people in Maastricht decided to complete the fortifications of Vauban on their own, which were built on the outside of the city wall. It was necessary; the successful French cannon attack proved that. Let's take a look at the works. Walking is healthy.

7. The reinforcements in north and south.

Very wide canals were dug on the outside of the city wall on the north and south sides of Maastricht.

In peacetime, they were filled with sheep droppings, but in wartime the wide canals were filled with water from the nearby small river Jeker.

That way, they looked like lovely elongated ponds, but in fact they were camouflaged city canals. No cannon was able to hit a city wall several times in the same spot from such a long distance. Driving through the water with heavy cannons and shooting from there was impossible because of the mud. So the enemy had to wade through the water to the city wall with their rifles, heavy barrels of gunpowder, and an extra heavy aversion.

In the middle of the water, they had dug trenches that were invisible from the surface. The intention was that enemy soldiers would suddenly disappear into these depths. Even if they could swim, the bullets in their cartridge bags would become soaked and unusable. Bullet shells were paper tubes in those days!

The defenders hoped that the soaked enemy soldiers would decide that it was better to go back. To encourage them more, they shot them from the city wall with musket bullets as thick as cherry bonbons.

8. The defenses in the west.

Wide 'ponds' to keep the enemy cannons away could not be constructed on the west side of the city. There is a large hill, and the water would simply drain away. That is why they dug a dry moat hundreds of meters before the city wall. The enemy would have to climb down into the moat with their heavy cannons and then bring them up again to get close to the city wall. But the brick walls of the dry moat were two meters thick, and on both sides there was a large number of embrasures with bunkers behind it. Of course, the defenders would shoot violently during the moving of the cannons. Therefore, the enemy soldiers first had to jump into the moat without guns to throw explosives into the shooting holes. That was only possible if they were very poisoned by adrenaline and therefore completely crazy.

But that was no problem because everyone in their family was hungry. The communication during their childhood was usually done by swear words and ear figs. They had to fight off everyone in the big family for every crust of bread. So their adrenaline was top-quality.

They were given a beautiful uniform, but after they arrived at the front, their high adrenaline level rose even more due to fatigue, homesickness, lovesickness, rain showers, wet socks, and lack of toilet paper.

At that moment, their brains were so paralyzed by adrenaline that they were very willing to jump into the dry canal, accompanied by aggressive trumpet noise, for the fatherland, the banner, and the beloved king.

This was a damn shame, because without adrenaline they were undoubtedly very nice guys. Now while jumping into the dry moat, they were shot from out of the loopholes by a hail of bullets with accompanying ear-splitting noise. If the enemy couldn't

be stopped that way, the defenders of Maastricht had another attraction on the program. In the walls of the dry canal, there were at some places high gates. There were no doormats lying in front of them but rectangular pits with walls lined with bricks a few meters deep.

Over those pits were drawbridges. They did not go up in emergency situations, but went down. Then the gates opened with a slam and horses with horsemen armed with long lances came out. It was fervently hoped that the enemy, with his last remnant of useful intelligence, would make the decision to run away. It is better to lose your honor than to lose your life, although adrenaline patients may have difficulty understanding this.

If in spite of everything the enemy managed to make a hole somewhere in the walls of the dry canal, they would discover that the tunnels inside (nine miles!) were closed off here and there by very thick oak doors. According to soldierly custom and under the influence of adrenaline, the intruders of course would kick against it. But on the other side of these doors, the defenders could light a fuse. The fuse went through a brick tube under the door to a charge of gunpowder just under the feet of the unsuspecting attackers. The builders of the fortifications had set up this present in advance. How the enemy would be surprised!

9. The reinforcement in the east.

On the east side of Maastricht, the city wall was sufficiently strong. From that side, you could only conquer the city district Wijck. Once you had gone to all that effort, your reward was a beautiful view of the Maas with its church towers (see left, outside the picture).

As beautiful as that view is, especially at sunset, enemies usually wanted more: namely, to rob and murder the residents of the city center as their red-hot adrenaline-fueled brains prescribed. Therefore, an enemy army had to go over the Romanesque bridge. But that bridge had a wooden section (nowadays metal) that the defenders of Maastricht would collapse in wartime.

And so century after century, everybody was busy with fighting against the aggression-producing adrenaline of others without asking where all this adrenaline came from and how to prevent the production of it to begin with.

This is a good sample of stupid symptom control and ignoring the cause. When will we humans learn from the past? Let's take a big towel and cry out our shame.

10. The Fort St. Pieter is being built.

The most important contribution to combating these symptoms was the construction of Fort St. Pieter on the northern edge of the St. Pietersberg in 1701 and 1702. Thanks to that fort, an enemy could not shoot cannons from the St. Pietersberg to the city anymore, or to the gates. The owner of the piece of ground on which the fort had to be built was the bishop of Liège. He stubbornly said "no" when the people of Maastricht asked him whether they could build a fort on that spot. He probably earned a lot of money by selling tickets for places of honor in heaven and possibly wanted to build a nice castle on St. Pietersberg from the proceeds. The view is beautiful there. What did he care about the thousands of frightened people from Maastricht who wanted to build a fort on his land?

But the people in Maastricht started building the fort without his permission.

The bishop was furious. He sent letters to everyone, but they laughed about him behind his back. He sat on velvet pillows, believed in fairy tales, and did not understand the people of Maastricht, who for centuries had been the target of wild adrenaline sufferers, crazed by hunger.

Maastricht was besieged fifteen times in its history and conquered six times. Once the Spaniard Parma killed almost all of the citizens of the city. According to Professor Wikipedia, only a few hundred people remained alive. The spoiled bishop would have been better to keep his mouth shut.

11. The working of the fort.

The bricks for the fort were baked in the open. This was apparently done very quickly, because the first version of the fort was built within two years by men, women, and children. It has eight loopholes for cannons along with several cannons on the original flat roof (see photo: the green line under the three arched windows). With that, future besiegers around the town could be shot in the back. This would quickly give the enemy the idea of attacking the fort first.

But the outside of the fort consisted of a two-meter-thick brick wall with 110 loopholes for muskets. Four hundred and fifty soldiers worked there during wartime. They had probably fled from home because of poverty, moldy bread, and woodlice. So they were also full of adrenaline, which turned them into impatient barbarians. Half of the soldiers would wait with their muskets beside the shooting holes for orders while the others were busy loading as many muskets as possible.

The pentagonal fort was divided into sections, and there was an officer with a whistle in each section. If he blew on that, all the shooters of that part had to shoot simultaneously through the shooting holes, causing great bangs. Thick clouds of smoke lit by orange fire rays would then spit outside. The most important thing was to scare the enemy. The whistling of the bullets was also part of that. Actual hits took too long and were therefore not the main goal.

After these rounds, the enemy knew that it would take at least a minute to reload the muskets and shoot again. Not at all!! Surprise!! The shooters immediately had another loaded musket in their hands. The whistle would sound, and the next shot came a few seconds after the first round. Then followed the next one and the next. The enemy had to think that they were using a magical weapon that could fire so quickly in succession. The defenders of the fort hoped that the bewildered enemy would withdraw behind the bushes to sing softly the lament:

"Oh, I wish… I'd stayed home… with my mom…"

(The more mature reader will understand that this is a joke of the author.) By the way, all the trees and shrubs on the St. Pietersberg had to be cut down during wartime so that hiding was impossible.

Usually there was a canal with water around this kind of fort. Its purpose was to prevent the enemy from arriving unhindered at the thick oak entrance door with unfriendly intentions. But in areas with hills and valleys, that water flows away. In such cases, dry canals are used, as with this fort. These canals were filled with a thick layer of round boulders, which you could only stumble across with great difficulty. In the meantime, these stumbling figures could be easily shot.

A dry canal also had an additional advantage: You could use hand grenades there. These were like cast-iron snowballs filled with gunpowder and with a burning wick.

They were rolled out of the lowest shooting holes, which slanted downward. Because there was no water in the canal, the wicks were not extinguished.

On the original flat roof of the fort, there were not only cannons but also mortars. These were small cannons that looked like church bells mounted upside down on a wooden base. There was no clapper in it, but a paper bag with gunpowder. On the mortar grenade were rings by which it could be lifted by two soldiers and lowered into the short barrel.

The mortar shells used on the fort were cast-iron spheres with a diameter of 14 inches. They were hollow, had a wall thickness of 1.5 inches, and were filled with gunpowder.

Today, you can still see a few of them in the fort, without gunpowder of course. It is estimated that an empty mortar weighs a hundred pounds. (I never dared to lift one, for which I later received a compliment from my doctor.) Filled with gunpowder, their weight was maybe a hundred and forty pounds. Using the formula $\pi = 22/7$ and with a table of the specific weights, I was able to calculate the weight at the age of 16, reluctantly but exactly.

I wished they had taught me how to find a suitable girlfriend instead of forcing me to spend years and years on these kinds of vaguely interesting side issues, which were only important for a handful of engineers.

I continue.

Through a hole at the bottom of the mortar cannon, the gunpowder was lit by a stick with a burning fuse. The noise must have been terrible. Due to the short barrel, mortar grenades flew through the air with a arc. Very handy to shoot over a city wall, but from the fort, they were shot over the dry canal to the St. Pietersberg plateau. There was a wick sticking out of the mortar grenade that started to smolder immediately when the grenade was shot.

(This was not possible with cannonballs because of their long reach.)

Because the wicks were short, the mortar grenades exploded in the air, resulting in a lot of deaths. An understandable mindset because the enemy consisted of adrenaline-poisoned psychiatric patients who could no longer think clearly because of everything they had experienced in their slums and then in the army. They were extremely dangerous and were considered vermin.

This was, in fact, an injustice. It was not the enemy that was dangerous, but the adrenaline that drove them crazy. Patients and diseases are two different things. Killing a patient to fight his illness does not belong to the higher art of medicine.

For lovers of thinking, here is a small piece of philosophy.

Why don't we worry about the poverty and hunger of people who have had bad luck? Adrenaline drives them crazy, and after that, we bomb them.

Clever heads say that early intervention for these people costs a lot of tax money. That is absolutely correct. A lot of money. But what does the production of weapons cost over the course of many years, followed by an devastating war, revenge, liberation, and finally decades of reconstruction? This misery is much more expensive than handing out peanut butter sandwiches and some friendly words.

Not to mention the millions of deaths that this kind of shortsightedness costs every time.

12. Fear of the fort.

The fort had the primary function of being scary. That succeeded very well when Louis XV came to Maastricht, like his father did. Once again, there was hunger in the slums of Paris and the wild street boys had to be vented. But the king did not dare to attack the fort St. Pieter. That is why a battle was held outside the city against a collection of beautifully uniformed adrenaline patients from various foreign slums (1747).

It is said that some opposing generals fraternally sat in a café and laughed at all these poor idiots who were so hard working to kill each other. (It's just a rumor.)

Thanks to the adrenaline, the soldiers probably did not understand themselves, for whom, and for what they were shooting, like in a snowball fight on the playground of a school. The playground of this fight was the village of Lafelt near Maastricht (around 5,000 deaths, 10,000 wounded, and 3,000 dead horses in a few days).

13. The French Revolution.

The next French king, Louis XVI, was always getting fatter.
Everyone would have been happy for him, if his nationals were not becoming thinner at the same time.
The adrenaline of the people exploded in 1789: the French Revolution.
The task of the king and queen to play daddy and mommy to people of illiteracy was impossible, and they knew that. That is why they comforted themselves by making elegant dance steps to the rhythm of beautiful harpsichord music, by hunting rabbits in the park, or by lying in four-poster beds, squeezing extra-marital buttocks. They also occasionally lifted the glass and shouted, "Après nous le deluge!" or singing "Whiskey in the Jar" (with a French accent of course).
Of course, the rumors about this lifestyle also got through to the normal people, who were busy daily looking for something to eat. The king began to point to the horizon again.
"There lives the enemy," he cried. "He is the cause of your hunger. Go there and ruin everything, but please don't do it here."
But this time, something very strange happened. The French people no longer believed their king! They already knew his old magic trick. This time the people pointed at the king. He was designated as the cause of poverty, not any innocent 'enemy.'
(That of course was not entirely true either. What did such a crowned theatre-figure know? In fact, he was only the puppet of his credulous environment.)
This new conviction caused the French revolution.
The revolutionaries took the power into their own hands, and many nobles were beheaded with the guillotine. They should not have hacked off those heads; it would have been better to force these heads to start thinking and solve the eternal food problem. Instead of sending hungry soldiers to innocent enemies to shoot

them, you also can make an army from them of cheerfully singing farmers in attractive cowboy suits with spades and pitchforks. The girls like that as well! This is how you really tackle the problem.

But again, I am never asked anything.

14. The revolutionaries are coming.

The French revolutionaries wanted to free all of Europe from the nobility. These revolutionaries were also full of adrenaline. This time not because of a failed harvest, but now in fear of the neighboring countries. The nobility in those countries was extremely outraged that the French people had murdered their own king and many nobles. Desperately, they wondered how this was possible. Where did they get the guts? Everyone knew that the nobility was personally chosen by God and was solemnly blessed in the presence of small, fluttering, naked angels. There were even large paintings with gold frames from that sacred moment. Was there absolutely nothing holy anymore?

Many French nobility fled abroad. There, with the help of foreign monarchs, they attempted to form armies to force the brutal revolutionaries back to their adrenaline-causing dog houses. Since attack is the best defense, the revolutionaries were more or less forced to attack the nobility in many parts of Europe. They hoped that in the conquered countries the time would also be ripe for revolutions, so that they would be welcomed as liberators, but that was disappointing.

A demonstration after the restoration of the fort in 2007. It shows how the army of the nobles welcomed the French revolutionaries in Maastricht in 1793.

General de Miranda of the French revolutionary army was very surprised to discover how fiercely the town Maastricht was defended by the nobles. Most of the resistance came from Fort St. Pieter. He could not believe his ears. It was hopeless.

After a month, he decided to go back with his army to Paris.

There he saw very angry faces, and he was immediately fired. *Nom de patate avec mayonnaise!* A general who was not able to conquer a small city like Maastricht with an army of 15,000 soldiers!! The nobility throughout Europe must have cheered!

But immediately a new army was formed and sent to Maastricht in 1794, this time with 32,000 revolutionaries, led by General Kléber.

Looking at old engravings, it would not surprise me if this man could look back on a very difficult childhood. He shot the fort so heavily from out of the surroundings of Chateau Neercanne (near Maastricht) that one wall almost collapsed. But it didn't go fast enough for him, and because there was no deposit on cannonballs, the supply was running out.

Cannons in Fort St. Pieter. Weight approx. 5000 pounds. Barrels were for paper bags with gunpowder. Wooden wheels did not cause sparks.

General Kléber decided to make a super-explosion in the caves below the fort. As a result, he hoped, a part of St. Pietersberg would fly into the sky, hand in hand with the fort. But there was a problem. You cannot look through the ceiling in the caves to see whether you are under the fort. But the French had managed to get a map of the caves. This allowed them to point out with great certainty a thick column above which the fort was located. The column was surrounded by barrels full of gunpowder with a wick. After it was lit, the revolutionaries ran with bulging eyes of fear and with their hands on their ears, loudly panting to the cave exit. An underground rumbling could be heard outside, but the fort did not move an inch.

In the caves, it took a few days for the smoke to disappear. Then the revolutionaries could see that the thick column was gone. The ceiling had been turned into a large dome but had not collapsed, as they already had suspected. They made another interesting discovery. Looking at the map, it turned out that the fort was not above the disappeared column, but half a mile away. No worry; they had plenty of explosives. However, even after a second explosion (extra strong), the ceiling didn't collapse.

But after six weeks the nobles of Maastricht surrendered.

They were banned from of the city, poor like mice, but alive. Again, Maastricht was a French town.

15. Napoleon appears on the scene.

To make a long story short: After a few years, Napoleon became the leader of the French revolutionaries. He turned the gang of rioters into a real army and changed the nobility into refugees in large parts of Europe.

Casually he visited Maastricht, where he was offered a free tour in the caves.

(Or did he have to pay the entrance fee? Let's not worry about trivial matters. He was there.)

Napoleon wanted to free Europe from nobility, but the remedy was worse than the disease. A few million deaths later, Napoleon was taken prisoner of war by the Prussian mercenary troops who'd fought for the nobility. That happened in Paris, because they had chased him there. To the relief of the European nobility, he was imprisoned on the island of Elba in the Mediterranean Sea on April 28, 1814.

The Prussians went home again, but on the way back, a large number of them visited the bars of Maastricht, looking for women who liked the bed-sport.

A small number of those soldiers were more patient and visited the St. Pietersberg caves first. There they wrote their names on a wall with the date June 9, 1814.

16. Napoleon escapes!

To the great fright of the nobility, Napoleon escaped from the island of Elba after about seven months. He made landfall in the South of France. The French revolutionary army was still completely intact and cheerfully attacked the nobility again (1815).

In panic, the nobility of Maastricht built a new fort on the north side of the city: Fort Willem. The construction would take three long years, but hopefully Napoleon could be stopped somewhere along the way. ("Please sir, we are not yet ready!") (Joke).

This new fort consisted of a hill of clay, on which cannons stood. From there, it was possible to shoot unwanted (French revolutionary) troops in the back if they encircled the city. Around the hill was a dry canal with walls of two meters thick. In these walls were dozens of loopholes, and from the bunkers behind these walls, the defenders could shoot into the dry canal.

But in 1815, Napoleon was captured for the second time during the Battle of Waterloo in Belgium.

This time he was exiled to the island of St. Helena, far in the Atlantic. There he died in 1821. (By poisoning, it was whispered.)

Yet the construction of Fort Willem was completed.

17. More symptom-combat.

The French Revolution was caused by hunger, cold, diseases, and fleas. As a reminder: bitter poverty is life-threatening, causing adrenaline in the blood of the victims, which makes them dangerous. They are not called 'victims' or 'patients,' but were contemptuously called the 'riff-raff.'

Imagine: A psychiatrist calls his patients 'riff-raff.' This would be unthinkable, but most people use that name for adrenaline patients. Riff-raff should be destroyed, is usually said or thought. But in reality, they are patients who need to be treated quickly before they go completely mad and become life-threatening.

May I also say something, as a writer?

Instead of making weapons, it would be cheaper and safer to turn slums into healthy neighborhoods, with supermarkets full of food.

It is understood that the illiterate of the past were not able to do that, but what's stopping us today from making the whole world slum-free? In the new houses will be only grateful friends, who will diligently help with more improvements.

Back again from futuristic dreams to the world of the past.

Everyone was amazed that by the destructions of the French Revolution poverty had not disappeared, but had increased tenfold and the level of the adrenaline as well.

Due to the growing numbers of hotheads, everybody started to build fortresses and city walls, rather than combating poverty preventively.

Also the Fort St. Pieter was renovated. Four L-shaped bunkers were built around the outside of the dry moat, which were initially only accessible underground. (See picture.) The photo also shows the oak entrance door, which is seven centimeters thick. Furthermore, a double row of loopholes for muskets and large openings to get rid of the smoke from cannons. Shooting holes for cannons are right around the corners of the fort. You cannot see them in the picture, but they are really there.

A bunker with three arched 'skylights' for mortar shells was built on the flat roof of the fort. Twelve bunkers were also made there for twelve cannons with their crews.

The hunger was not combated.

18. The fort has to disappear.

Around 1880, grenades were invented that exploded on impact. The old fortresses could not withstand that. Fort St. Pieter was also disapproved by the ministry of Loud Bangs and was empty for a long time.

Around 1900, it was sold for a bargain price to a farmer, who was obliged to demolish it. He was allowed to keep the bricks. At first, he made stables from the four bunkers along the dry moat. He closed a number of loopholes in these bunkers and made doors and windows in them, at the request of the cows. Then the brave man began to demolish the seven cannon bunkers aimed at the river Maas. In the beginning, all went well, but then he got cramps in his right leg. He also had pain in his neck and shoulder. One day, he stopped demolishing. As a result, the fort remained 90 percent upright. This is fortunately, because now it is an impressive monument of backwardness full of exciting corridors, stairs, and antique cannons, but today without puddles of blood.

19. Tutoring by a cat.

Now the moment has arrived that I want to express my thanks to Tibi, a cat who once tutored me. This happened on a day I was phoned by a student.

He was on vacation with his girlfriend for a week. Because of the excitement, he had forgotten to feed his cat and asked whether I could do that. It was a very sweet animal. The student told me where he had hidden the key to his room. Shortly thereafter, I entered that room with a can of cat-food and a bottle of milk.

What I saw was indescribable. The cat immediately ran to me, hissing and huffing, and started to scratch my legs furiously, straight through the trouser legs.

The animal had thrown over two table lamps, there were towels on the floor, ripped books and newspapers, and a cat turd on the student's pillow was grinning at me.

Was this all the work of that 'sweet animal'?

That cat was perilous! I wanted to kick the beast, but luckily I changed my mind. In time I understood that adrenaline was bubbling in the animal when he realized that starvation was coming for him.

This poison made him dangerously aggressive, and his cat brain became unusable.

I gave him his food and cleaned up the worst of the mess. The next day, I went to visit the cat early to treat him to a can of cat food. We became great friends. Was that sweet animal the same monster as a day before?

How do people behave in such a situation?

Do we feed the poor at an early stage to prevent them from becoming crazy and dangerous by adrenaline poisoning? Nonsense!

Just bomb them.

20. At last school education.

With the disappearance of the nobility, democracy took over in many countries. Now everyone was allowed to contribute ideas about forming a government.

Because the many illiterate people did not even know how to hold a red pencil in a voting booth, education became compulsory in those areas (around 1900). Because power was given to the people, that people first had to be able to count to ten.

Committees were formed to compile the curricula. Because these notables were one-eyed in the land of the illiterate, they did not know the answer to the question: What shall we teach the children? Well, what? What would be important?

21. Jules Verne.

At that time the French writer Jules Verne came along. He showed what a fantastic world you can create if everyone uses their minds and collects in their brains many smart facts. The people in his books started to think first, and then they discussed their ideas with other people, under the eyes of the surprised readers.

He then described the wonderful results that this thinking produced. The titles of his books say enough:

From the Earth to the Moon, *20,000 Leagues Under the Sea*, *Journey to the Center of the Earth*, and *Around the World in 80 Days* (at that time, such a journey took years).

Jules Verne became world famous and undoubtedly influenced the inventors of the class schedules.

The teaching package of secondary schools in particular seem to have been designed by Jules Verne himself.

In a world full of people who could only produce farts and belches or walk drunk in the streets, arrogant figures with top hats and sanctimonious cowards, that curriculum was a large beam of light. Really a fantastic program.

Poverty and hunger, the cause of adrenaline and aggression, would certainly disappear now.

But it was already too late.

22. Again cannons.

Even before education had a chance to prevent hunger and poverty and thus the umpteenth adrenaline eruption, two world wars broke out. Poverty had not yet been dispelled, but the clever laws of physics that the people had learned in school were immediately used to make machine guns and cannons. Nobody came up with the idea that you could also make agricultural machines with that knowledge.

During the Second World War, a low bunker was built on the roof of Fort St. Pieter as a lookout.

At night, in good weather, hundreds, sometimes a thousand, English bombers flew over the city, several times a week, year after year. They were on their way to bomb German cities to calm the adrenaline sufferers, according to the psychological insight of the time. (Those insights, in my opinion, have hardly changed since then, thanks to the unchanged teaching programs, in which the word 'psychology' nowhere was to be found.)

I estimate that my parents and their five children had to run to the cellar at night about 600 times during the Second World War.

The English bombers were awaited and fired at by German fighter planes. From the bunker on the fort, the people of the Air Protect Services could see where the burning planes crashed. Sixty-one bombers crashed in a radius of 10 miles around Maastricht. The reader will understand that I strongly hate war, especially after the two-day liberation of a village to which we had fled. There we were with nine people and a barking sheepdog in the small cellar of a house that stood between two trenches. That meant hours of shivering and chattering teeth with fear.

To our great surprise, we survived that. We were liberated by an American tank division called "Hell on Wheels." Not a word of that was untrue.

I don't like to stir up all that misery. I already wrote a book about that. After five miserable years, the war was over. It had been so terrible (an estimated 70 million deaths) that people finally began to think about what might have caused it. Usually people don't, because why buy an umbrella when the rain is over? We humans are not that gifted. But this time, very strict tax laws were designed. They had to make sure that frustrated figures, who thought they had no other talent than collecting money, would stop with their dangerous hobby. This brings others great problems.

Top-heavy incomes were from that moment skimmed off so that others could get salary increases, social assistance, child allowance, and free education. As a result, the money infarcts disappeared, and the money kept rolling like oil in an engine. As a result, society in Europe could no longer get stuck, for the first time in history.

Had we now started an adrenaline-free period, without wars?

Almost, because adrenaline can also bubble up for reasons other than poverty and hunger.

23. The miracles of the school education!

In the end, the Jules Verne education produced great miracles.

The sickles were replaced by agricultural machines. The pill was invented, as well as hundreds of medicines. Almost any organ can be transplanted. Everyone drives a car, and at the moment, thousands of people are on planes seven miles above us. Man has even visited the moon. Central heating was invented, the bicycle bell, and the cat door. We have surpassed the fantasy world of Jules Verne hundreds of times.

Can we do now the next step?

24. Unexpected adrenaline outbreak.

No wonder school-education soon was declared sacred. But nobody realized that the brand-new education was (and is) an untested prototype, primitive like the first steam train. It requires children to sit on benches for years in silence and being obedient. Especially in high school, they are fattened with a heavy scientific stew such as: their own national language (for me Dutch), French, English, and German. (It was recommended to learn Greek and Latin as well, but I left the eating of those delicacies to others.)

Is that all?

No, we had to swallow algebra, geometry, arithmetic, chemistry, physics, history, geography, biology, economics, accounting, and public administration. This all was (is) rammed down the throat of the students without anesthesia. All with help of punishments, tutoring, poor grades, renewed exams, and the threat of boarding school (where I was for three years). Worst of all, students don't have time left to think. Thinking is called laziness. Facts and formulas should be eaten. All for our own good. Our mutilations were rewarded with a beautiful diploma.

By this well-intentioned Jules Verne school program, only the brain is trained. The brain, that's what it's all about, we are led to believe. Feelings are considered weeds to be destroyed, but are, in fact, a compass.

Without feelings, the brain can easily run wild and turn you into a dangerous, rational creep. Is the production of mutilated people—creeps—who have food three times a day the aim of our schools?

Isn't it time to put education into second gear?

What is wrong with happy people who don't need drugs?

Brains and feelings need each other to take crossbearings in order not to get lost. One corrects the other.

Am I the only one who's discovered that? Of course not. But why are others silent? Probably because they are more obedient than I am.

Ladies and gentlemen, do allow me to say these words: Hunger and poverty, have caused much adrenaline. With school education, this disappeared. But nobody could foresee that education itself would become an adrenaline-maker!

This insufficiently tested education has some severe side effects.

Even if only half of what I am saying here is true, then it would be nice to think about it, all together.

25. Help from professionals.

It would be good to have the sainted Jules Verne teaching programs from 1900 rewritten by real professionals, such as experienced psychotherapists and psychologists. They should control and adjust the teaching-programs every ten years to reduce crime, suicide, drug use, the wave of divorce, riots, and war threats. Personally, I think this is a beautiful thought, which one can contemplate for a long time—also you, reader!

I don't know everything!

But we haven't gotten that far yet, and so the ancient, blunt teaching-programs are incessantly and lovelessly pumped into the brains of students. This is accompanied by penalties, bad reports, homework, and retakes. Our class no longer wanted to let themselves be daily disapproved on the basis of standards devised by professionals from the past with good intentions. Should we continue to wait for improvements? We didn't. We spontaneously designed a new kind of education, without teachers:

"The trial-and-error education"

26. Trial-and-error education in practice.

(Some interesting examples)

In high school, we made an important discovery: If you play truant with a few boys, it is truancy. If you skip school with an entire class at the same time, it is a misunderstanding. Occasionally we treated ourselves to such well-earned misunderstandings.

Once we took a trip with the whole class to Fort St. Pieter and to the caves deep beneath. To enter, we climbed, eager to learn, upward against the side of the old fort with thirty-two boys. That wall was damaged by cannonballs from the time of the French Revolution. (Today it is restored. This story is set in 1949.)

Due to the lack of bricks here and there, there were holes in the wall that could be used as stairs. It took a lot of courage, because the fort was high, but we would rather drop to our death than be a coward. (How did we stupid idiots get that idea?!!)

At that period, there was a restaurant next to the fort. If one of the waitresses saw us, there would be a big alarm and our nice trip would be canceled. Fortunately, the wall on which we climbed up was not visible from the restaurant.

On the roof of the fort, we went back down by a stone staircase into the inside the fort. Of course, it was a detour, but we had no keys to use the main entrance. Downstairs, the cold corridors are mysteriously lit by many shooting-holes in the thick walls. There is also a well on the same floor. Because the surface of the water is forty meters deep, the well is actually an empty tube made of bricks, comparable to an old factory chimney. If you throw a stone into the well, it takes four seconds before you hear 'splash' in the depth. The gate next to the well gives access to the spiral staircase around the tube, which didn't have a handrail.

Just above the water, the stairs swing in another direction, and so we arrived in the 'basement' of the fort. It consists of some high limestone corridors with an access to the caves.

In the past, soldiers and ammunition could be brought secretly into the fort through those caves. But in that way also an enemy could come in. That is why there is a brick tube about three yards long between the 'basement' of the fort and the caves. An enemy could only crawl through it on his own, lying on his belly. Enemies don't like that. Certainly not in the darkness, because with the draft in that tube, any candle would be blown out.

It took a long time for thirty-two boys to crawl through the narrow tube.

But in the end, we came into the 'collapsed area' of the caves. This is where the French revolutionaries tried, in vain, to destroy the fort with a super-explosion in the caves (1794).

There is still a lot of debris there, and we had to crawl over and under it.

It is very dangerous to get lost in a cave with, at that time, 150 miles of corridors. But two boys claimed that they knew the way, so we went with them confidently. After an hour, our two 'guides' had a surprise for us. They said they were unfortunately lost.

"Lost???"

"Yes, sorry, sorry!"

"Sorry, sorry? Damn!"

Lost in the caves!! With a whole class of truants!!

Of course, nobody knew that we were in the caves. How long would it take before someone got the idea to look for us here?

We might have to sit there in the dark for a few days and nights, green from hunger and shivering with cold. This would also have an unfavorable impact on our transition reports. We already had such a hard time with the teachers, who called us 'the first war wave.' They regarded our class as a natural disaster. We thought the same of the teachers, who, with help of punishments and bad school reports, forced us to learn a largely useless range of facts from the *fin de siècle*, for which we actually had no time.

After discovering that we were lost, we decided to ration the light. We had four flashlights with us. In a hurry, we walked and crawled further in the light of one flashlight, in a direction that hopefully would be the right one. After a long search, our 'guides' accidentally found the tube in the wall. We crawled through it and reached the spiral staircase. There we switched on all the lights again. That was necessary, because the stairs were as high as a twelve-story building. We climbed the steps with the last of our light, and with our last bit of breath we came upstairs.

At that moment, we heard the barking of dogs. Probably one of the waitresses had seen us and told her boss that there were boys in the fort again. He had patiently waited until we came up and then sent dogs at us. As paratroopers, we jumped one after the other out of four large shooting holes. During the jump, we discovered how high it was there. But on the other hand, we had luck because the dogs, with their big mouths, did not dare to jump down, so we ran away, limping in pain.

Fourteen days later, the result of the transitional exam came. From the 32 boys in our class, 16 failed their exam. I had very beautiful marks for drawing and gymnastics, but unfortunately also twelve marks of the worst sort. When my father saw my report, he thought it was high time to send me to a strict boarding school.

27. No light in the caves.

At the boarding school I became friends with Tom, who turned out to be very interested in Fort St. Pieter. Because I knew the way there, I promised to give him a tour during the next holiday. There were more interested boys, so we went in with five persons in the Christmas holiday.

This time we did not crawl up against the damaged wall, which was high and perilous, but we entered through one of the large cannon shooting-holes. Under them were handy holes in the wall (before the restoration) which we used as stairs. We didn't have to climb that high, but the disadvantage was that the shooting-holes were closer to the restaurant. Hopefully none of the severe waitresses would see us.

The inner part of the fort (near the well) is not lit by the dim light of the shooting-holes. There it is pitch dark. Because we were not going into the caves, I had only brought a small flashlight.

We were barely inside when we heard the thick oak entrance door from the restaurant into the fort open with a lot of noise. Apparently, somebody had seen us going inside.

We heard two male voices, probably from the owner and a waiter. They certainly did not come to welcome us with a bunch of flowers, so we ran away as quickly as possible. With the help of the flashlight, I ran with Tom to the inner part of the fort, to the well, and the spiral staircase. Quickly we went downstairs, wondering where the three others had gone. Fortunately, one of them knew the way in the fort. After a descent of about twenty-five steps, we stood still, and I turned off the light.

The core of the spiral staircase was an empty stone shaft, with water in the depth.

Because of its age, there were holes in the shaft, and when you looked down over the edge, you saw the light through those holes when people were walking on the spiral staircase with a flashlight.

So we stood silently in the dark. Undoubtedly the two men would be bent over the edge at that moment to look and listen. Fortunately, I didn't have to explain anything to Tom, an experienced boarding school boy. We were close to one of these holes, and we heard the men talking and cursing. To our great shock, we heard the sound of their footsteps and realized they were coming down the stairs! We nearly started to sweat of fear.

In the neat Roman Catholic Higher Citizens School for Boys (just the name smells of narrow-mindedness), it was fairly common, so shortly after the war, that the adrenaline-filled teachers slapped the students on the face if they didn't simulate enough interest for the stuff they had to swallow.

What would await us if we fell into the hands of these two unclear figures in such a remote place? Their frustrations, caused by many failed pursuits in the fort, would rain down on us with interest. Walking farther down in the dark on the worn stairway without a handrail was very dangerous, since on average, the steps were about 16 inches high, but if we used the flashlight, they could see us through the holes.

We couldn't do more than fervently hope that the men would turn around any moment, assuming they were mistaken. But they got closer and closer.

With racing hearts, we stood with our bellies pressed against the brick shaft. A beam of light came around the corner... just behind our backs... and then they stopped...

"They are not here," we heard from one of them, and they went back upstairs. It was as if we had won the lottery!! What a relief!! Upstairs, they were shouting for certainty in the well that they would send dogs after us. After that, it became very quiet.

The good news was that the other three boys had had enough time to escape through a shooting-hole. The bad news was that we didn't dare go back upstairs. We had to go farther into the depths, where a mountain of problems was waiting.

The very first problem was my small flashlight. Would the battery survive such a long journey? We needed a lot of time to go through the rubble of the collapsed area to the undamaged corridors.

From there, we had to walk to another exit. It was closed with a wooden door, but the lock could be opened from the inside without a key. Fortunately, I knew the way to that gate. Because I had become interested in the caves, some boys (who used a kite rope to keep from getting lost) had taught me the way to that exit. That happened during the summer vacation before I went to boarding school.

Hopefully I could find the way to that gate without a kite rope, but certainly I did not feel very sure. That's why I reluctantly went down the stairs with Tom.

We crawled through the brick tube and ended up in the middle of the large chunks of stone in the collapse area. You hardly could get through.

I decided not to spare the flashlight, because the chance of getting lost was greatest here. (The photo is from a much later date. We had other things in our mind than taking pictures).

Fortunately, the three escaped boys could tell the authorities where they should look for us if we didn't come home that night.

We climbed and crawled with sweaty faces over and under the blocks of stone until we arrived at a place where a huge rock had fallen. It was the size of a ship-container and was stuck between the walls of a corridor. I was happy when I saw that block, because it proved that we were on the right path. But I wasn't really happy.

The space under the block was so low that you had to lie flat to crawl underneath. This was accompanied by the ripping sound of your clothes. Especially in the middle of the block, it took a lot of self-control not to panic. You felt as if you were lying on a guillotine. This was the first time for Tom, but he was damn good and followed in silence.

When we were finally able to walk upright, in the corridors outside the collapsed area, it turned out that we had asked too much of the flashlight. It was still burning, but very faintly. We decided to save that last bit of light as a reserve. Fortunately, Tom had a lighter with him, and we used it.

But the flame of the lighter became smaller and smaller, and finally it went out! For a moment, we had it very stuffy.

While trying to get the lighter burning again, I discovered that the sparks from the flint gave a bright white light. Because I knew the way there, I wanted to try to walk on with help of those sparks. What else I could do?

The environment was briefly illuminated by each spark. Then I was thinking. What did I see? I saw... that the corridor made a turn to right. Ah! Then we were probably there... Another spark to check... Yes, it was right. After that, I took Tom by the arm, and we took ten careful steps in the dark. Another spark. To our surprise, this system worked. We walked on sparks!!

Only at crossings did I use the flashlight briefly.

Our speed was probably three hundred yards per hour, but in the end, we came out through the wooden gate. A long walk to civilization followed, again in the dark, because the winter sun was already at home.

The three boys, waiting in the bedroom of one of them, were relieved when we appeared after a few hours. If we had arrived an hour later, they would have been asking for help, although they did not know where. They had indeed jumped out of the fort's shooting holes when the two men were roaring into the well. It had been an interesting afternoon, humorous and yet fun, but I'd had enough of the fort and the caves for the first hundred years.

28. In love in the caves.

In the summer holidays of that same year, I fell in love with a girl. (Dear reader, may I introduce her to you? Her name was Mariette.)

In those days, when the pill did not exist, having a girlfriend just for a hobby was a phenomenon against which all worldly and ecclesiastical authorities barked unanimously long and loud. With such a girl (on high heels), climbing up the wall of a fort was so far removed from the prevailing pattern of thought that Mariette would immediately start to think that I was psychologically disturbed. That had to be prevented at all cost.

But fortunately, something special had happened!

When I was in boarding school, some of my former classmates had made a grand discovery. The official cave entrance, by which daily guides took people in, was a green-painted iron door. This surly door was opened in the morning by the first

guide with a key and closed in the evening by the last guide with a key. During the rest of the day, the door was closed, but... not locked! What a discovery!! You could just walk in there during the day. If only we had known earlier!! If normal people opened that door, they looked into a black tunnel and they didn't want to go any farther. (Since the arrival of the GSM with a built-in flashlight, the door is always locked securely.)

Now that I knew that the door was open during the day, I dared to ask Mariette if she would like to visit the caves with me. To my surprise, she said, "Yes!"

We cycled to the center of the town, where I, out of sight of my parents, took a flashlight from my attic room, and we drove to the cave entrance.

When the iron door closed behind us and we had taken the first three steps into the tunnel, I discovered how stupid you become if you have not learned enough algebra. I had completely forgotten to check whether the battery was loaded. It was almost empty. I told Mariette that our eyes still had to get used to the light, but that would improve soon. In reality, I did not believe my own words, and I was furious with myself.

Indeed, when we came to the end of the tunnel, where the actual limestone quarry begins, that was also the end of the battery.

I asked Mariette if she had anything flammable with her.

"Yes! A pocket diary."

"Can I tear a leaf out of it?"

It was allowed.

She also had a lighter with which I set fire to page:

'January 1, 1952.'

In that light, we quickly walked about ten yards.

Because I had walked through the caves with Tom on sparks, these burning papers were a great luxury. Mariette had no reason to complain.

Moments later, the following page was torn out.

Everything went entirely according to plan.

Of course, by the end of May (in the planner), we had to turn around. The rest of the year was needed for the way back. I kept the pages with titles (Very High Honored Learned Sir) (what an idiot must you be to let someone call you that?) plus the pages with the birthdays of the royal family as a reserve. With that, we could walk a few hundred meters extra.

When we at mid-April arrived at a crossing, we saw a group of people approaching in the corridor on the left, fairly close by, with a guide in front who was carrying a gasoline lamp. Fortunately, there was a dead-end niche in the corridor to our right where we quickly hid. Hopefully, the group would not walk past this niche, because there was no time to find a better place. The light became brighter, but luckily the people went to another corridor and then it became dark.

Just before I wanted to light a page again, I saw a small red light burning in front of me, about four yards away, in the pitch-black darkness. I stood still, looked at the light, squeezed Mariette in her arm (maybe it was her bosom by mistake), and whispered near where her ear was, "There is someone smoking a cigarette in the dark."

But that 'someone' had already heard us. He turned on his flashlight, which gave about 200 times more light than that stupid thing I'd used.

Probably it was a mushroom grower (still working there at that time) who had walked along with the group of cave visitors. Apparently, he had changed his mind, stopped, and was now, in order to save batteries, smoking the rest of his cigarette in the dark.

When he saw two stony ghosts in the beam of his light, he was scared to death. He started shouting and cursing, and he asked our names. Of course, we gave him wrong names. He would go to the police, he growled.

"Get out of here! Immediately out!"

In the light-beam from his lamp, we could walk about 25 yards. There was a corner, and we had to use the planner again. Finally, we reached the iron door and the redeeming daylight.

What should have been a romantic afternoon ended in this silly retreat.

A week later, I was back at the boarding school again and received a letter from Mariette. I quickly opened the envelope and started to read with great interest. What did she write? She wrote that she was ending her relationship with me.

Damn! Life always brings surprises, but always the wrong ones. Five years of war, weeks in a children's home, months in a hospital, a year in a sanatorium, the boarding school, and now this reward from Mariette.

Dear readers, I think that self-pity is now gradually allowed. I am not made of stainless steel.

29. Becoming a guide in caves and fort.

Many, many years later, after my retirement as a teacher at an art school, I didn't have enough money to pay alimony (I was divorced for the second time). Therefore, I obliged myself to sit down every day for one hour at a table with a notepad in front of me, just to think. How to get money? Every ridiculous idea was noted and reviewed the next day. After a few weeks, the coin had fallen! Become a cave guide! Of course, it was also a ridiculous idea, but I thought it was a great fit for me!

After a job interview with the director of the Tourist Office, he introduced me to Eduard, the head of the guides. He would teach me the way underground.

Before Eduard did so, I was first tested by him. At least I got that feeling.

In an above-ground guide room, where visitors can buy tickets, he told the most horrible stories about counting the cash register, the caprices of the alarm system, the problems with the computer, and the calculation of group-discounts. He pointed out the doors through which the tourists were allowed to go to the toilet. He demonstrated how to provide gasoline lamps with new socks, how to fill and light them, and where the fire extinguisher hung (nowadays, electric lamps are used).

He showed me brochures in various languages, including Japanese. He also spoke about pink, yellow, and white coupons, about lists that had to be filled in daily, and about a counter to count customers. After this, he paused to see what my reaction was to this horrific story. But even an ice cream seller has to fill in papers till late into the night. If I was too lazy for that, I'd better go to a retirement home.

When Eduard noticed that I wasn't broken, he was reassured and lit a gasoline lamp.

On my way to the cave entrance (North caves) a few hundred meters farther on, I enjoyed the view of the city from St. Peter's mountain. From now on, I would see this for free with every tour.

Eduard said that Maastricht has around one hundred guides. Fifty are available for city tours. The other half works underground in the caves, in the fort or in the casemates. After we entered the caves through the iron door, we took a tour through the corridors.

How was it possible that I once knew the way here, at least in a small part of the corridor system? To my surprise, I discovered my own name on a wall, with the year 1952, exactly fifty years ago!! I had not been here since and had forgotten a lot. There also I saw the name Bert, my friend, who later married my sister.

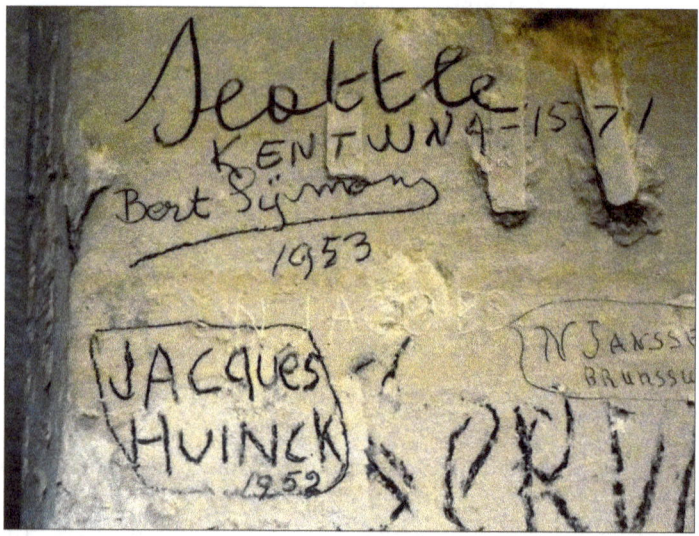

When we came back to the starting point, we made the same rounds again. Now I had to show the way, and of course I was lost within a minute. Edward showed me the different landmarks: a hole, a deep scratch, a name, a bend. You don't have more support there. The next day I had to come back, and we were underground for two hours again. He gave me lessons for many days. Because it was winter, there were few visitors.

Finally, I was allowed to lead the way with the lamp. At each crossing I stood still for a few seconds until Eduard stood beside me. That was very important, because the points of his shoes, which I looked unobtrusively at, usually pointed in the right direction. To my surprise, I did not get lost this time, although it was clear that in the long run, I also had to know the way without Eduard's shoes. I finally succeeded, and I felt very happy.

This happiness collapsed when Eduard gave me the following order:

"Now walk that same round again, but in the opposite direction."

Already after a hundred meters, I was lost. I was perplexed. Everything suddenly looked completely different, different light, different shadows, so I had to learn this version too.

Slowly it made me crazy, but a few weeks later, Eduard thought that I knew the road enough to walk through the caves alone to gain experience. He advised me to do this more often from then on. I had to report it to one of the guides and later report to the same guide that I was outside again. This was to prevent me being locked up a whole night in the caves, without anyone knowing that. At home, only Pim the cat was waiting for his food and for me (in that order).

As I walked there on my own, impressed by the incredible silence, the darkness and the loneliness, I saw monks jumping away in the side corridors, their faces hidden under black hoods.

It turned out to be the shadows of walls and pillars. After this, I heard a slight chirp. Eduard had told me what that was: bats that were making love. (How can these ugly animals fall in love with each other?)

They came to hibernate in the winter when there are no more mosquitoes outside. Mostly they are hanging on the ceiling, preferably in high corridors and in areas where no people came.

Shortly thereafter, I saw white ghosts. What now again? The ghosts shuffled slowly in my direction. It turned out to be about seven women from India, in long, white robes and with white headscarves. Their guide was invisible because of his dark jacket.

Then came the biggest shock of that day: the discovery that I'd lost the way.

For a moment I felt panic. What now? Eduard had not taught me that! I thought about it, put the lamp on the floor and thought again. I then walked with my spare flashlight into a corridor, but in a way that I still could see the light of the gasoline lamp.

There was nothing recognizable. Then back to the gasoline lamp and into another corridor. In the third corridor, I recognized a drawing on a wall and knew the way again. Eduard would never know that I was lost. He might extend the course by a few weeks. All the while, I would not receive a salary, while I needed every penny.

My ex-wife's lawyer probably used to be an obedient schoolboy who amputated his feelings without any protest, which changed his childhood in a missed chance. After this discovery he felt himself indignant and maybe got a lot of adrenaline in his blood and started to hate everybody.

No doubt he immediately saw his opposite in me, I think, and that probably explained why he seemed to be using me as his personal lightning rod. As a result, my furniture consisted of a table, a plastic garden chair, and a mattress on a cement floor. I also had to pay much alimony. But the thought that the children were not left in a plundered house was a comfort to me.

Now many years later, I have fully recovered myself in every sense. Hopefully the poor lawyer can say the same. But when I became a cave guide, I was still deeply in financial difficulties.

Eduard gave me a big file with papers on which were escribed all kinds of events that had taken place in the caves over the centuries. By this, new guides can compile a field-bouquet of stories to their own taste. As a result, the stories of the guides are all different.

Finally, the exam came, which was controlled by Eduard and the director of the tourist office.

To my fright, the tourists I had to show around were Americans, so the exam had to be done in English. But with success!

Later I also gave guided tours in the caves of Zonneberg (another part of the St. Pietersberg) and in the Fort St. Pieter.

Since 2002 I have made about 4000 people per year laugh. Now (18 years later) that totals more than 70,000 laughing people! Of course, there are also dramatic stories to tell, for example about people who used to get lost in the caves and who did not survive. But this no longer happens due to better controls and better doors!

My colleagues are special figures, very nice, and there is a good bond between us all.

Paying alimony has enriched me very much! It forced me to do this cave-'work.'

Ladies and gentlemen, this is the end of the tour, which lasted much longer than usual. Hopefully you liked it a bit. I am now going outside, and if you want, you can come with me!

30. Finally.

Finally, we found each other!
Christina Bloem (68)
Jacques Huinck (70)
now guides in this cave 2005
Don't write on the walls.

In the meantime, I got to know Christina through the Internet. (Where else?) (Having job interviews in dark cafés during a roaring music bombardment and in a half drunken state leads to nothing, I quickly discovered.) She was interested in my job, and very soon she also wanted to become a guide in the caves.

Because of her work as a journalist for a walking magazine, she often took long walks, and I began to walk with her. She already walked several times to Santiago via different routes and wanted to do this again soon. Her question was if I wanted to walk along with her to Santiago.

"Sweetheart, I like you very much, but put that idea out of your head. I may be crazy, but I'm certainly not that crazy! Walking days and days with a heavy backpack through Spain? Sorry, I don't see myself doing that."

31. Walking 750 miles through Spain!

Why not, actually? When after many centuries, the time came that the proud carriage was suddenly deeply ridiculed by the high-speed train, everybody had to reorient by trial and error. May be this walk in 2007 had something to do with it. But we have the feeling that we are on the right track and wish everyone good luck.

The author

Jacques Huinck, born in 1935 in Maastricht, the Netherlands, was an independent photographer and filmmaker. He won the Prix Nièpce in Paris for his photos, received a travel grant to Hollywood for his first film and made 36 short features for a psychological faculty. He taught at the Maastricht Art Academy for 26 years. After his retirement he worked 18 years as a guide in the caves and the antique fortress St. Pieter in Maastricht.

In the Second World War he experienced the liberation (by Americans) in the basement of a house that stood between two trenches.

After the war, he was trained as a photographer and filmmaker in bombed Germany and became acquainted with the mentality of the former enemy. He couldn't stop remain interested in the cause of this global disaster and wrote his conclusions (with humor) in this book.

The publisher

> **He who stops getting better stops being good.**

This is the motto of novum publishing, and our focus is on finding new manuscripts, publishing them and offering long-term support to the authors.
Our publishing house was founded in 1997, and since then it has become THE expert for new authors and has won numerous awards.

Our editorial team will peruse each manuscript within a few weeks free of charge and without obligation.

You will find more information about
novum publishing and our books on the internet:

www.novumpublishing.com

Rate this book on our website!

www.novumpublishing.com

www.ingramcontent.com/pod-product-compliance
Lightning Source LLC
Chambersburg PA
CBHW050705160426
43194CB00010B/2011